WINGS

A 90-DAY COMPANION JOURNAL to CULTURE OF GRATITUDE

Special free bonus gift for you

To help you attain more gratitude, there are FREE BONUS RESOURCES for you at:

https://ericosae-twum.org

ERIC OSAE-TWUM

2024   EKOT NUTURING.ORG

Foreword by Rev. Kevin D. Cook CCBW

For permissions requests, contact: Eric Osae-Twum at: http://ericosae-twum.org

EKOT NURTURING PARADIGMS

ISBN: 979-8-9901151-3-2

Printed in the U.S.A.

Visit http://ericosae-twum.org for more information about this book and the author.

Cover design by Cimons Technologies

First Printing: August 2024

Dedication:

To my dear mom, Charity, whose passing led to the birthing of this piece. You taught me how to stay strong in the face of adversity, and more importantly, I watched you live this through the strength and courage you continuously exhibited while raising us. I miss you!

Foreword:

When Eric told us, "You are our father and our mother, and you have no choice in the matter. I must learn from you," it was not just a statement of respect but a declaration of a journey we were about to embark on together. This profound moment came after I had shared a deeply personal truth with him, a secret kept between God and me until then. It began a relationship defined by trust, growth, and the shared pursuit of spiritual depth.

Our paths crossed with Eric and Stella at the Life on Fire Abundance Conference (a divinely orchestrated meeting) in July 2021. My wife (Kathy) and I were there to find new directions for my ministry, Lasting Impact, but we found something more: a friendship that would challenge and enrich us in ways we hadn't anticipated. This bond was forged not just in shared beliefs but in the genuine expressions of gratitude that Eric and Stella lived by every day.

Their gratitude is not passive; it's a vibrant, living practice that extends into every aspect of their lives. Every coaching session with them begins the same way: "How are you?" I would ask, and their reply, without fail, was always, "We are well by God's grace." This simple exchange encapsulates a heart of thankfulness that they live out daily, reminding us of the power and simplicity of gratitude.

Eric and Stella didn't stop at being students of life and leadership coaching; they embarked on the path to becoming coaches themselves. Their desire to guide and inspire others is a testament to their commitment to growth and service. This dedication is evident in everything they do, from how they've embraced their personal development to their efforts to launch and support a Christian school. They have indelibly impacted their community, demonstrating what living a life of gratitude and purpose means.

The devotional you are about to read is a culmination of Eric's dream and our shared experiences. It is an invitation to explore gratitude as a feeling and a way of life that can profoundly transform how we see the world and interact with others. Through these pages, Eric and Stella hope to share their lessons, the joy they've discovered in serving others, and the peace from a heart full of gratitude.

As you delve into this devotional, let the stories and reflections guide you to a deeper understanding of gratitude's power. May you find, as we have, that a grateful heart is the key to unlocking a more fulfilling, joyous life.

We welcome you on this journey of transformation and discovery, inspired by Eric, Stella, and the countless lives they've touched. Here's to finding the joy of living with gratitude and purpose.

Preface

Dear Reader,

On a quiet afternoon in February 2022, a phone call brought the world around me to a standstill. It was the news of my mother, Charity Agyemang's, passing. In the wake of this profound loss, which followed forty years after my father's departure, I embarked on an unexpected journey. It was not overshadowed by grief but rather enlightened by a newfound sense of gratitude.

In the stillness that followed, I reflected not on the loss but on the life she lived.

- How could I honor the resilience of a woman who single-handedly shaped four decades of our lives?

- Could gratitude be the key to healing the void left by her absence?

These musings became the seeds of the devotional in your hands. It's a tribute to the transformative power of gratitude – a journey from appreciating life's simple joys to finding strength in adversity.

Why a 90-day devotional? Because true transformation requires time. I hope and pray that this devotional is repeated within the four cycles of 90 days per year; gratitude becomes more than a practice for you – it becomes a sanctuary, a place of deep understanding and celebration of life, even in its passing moments.

This guide is a journey of the soul. It navigates through thankfulness, encounters everyday blessings, and reframes challenges as opportunities. It's about finding gratitude mixed with faith, culminating in a life lived fully and gratefully.

As you embark on this journey, I invite you to dive deep into each page. Engage with it, reflect on it, and let it be a mirror to your inner world and a window to joys yet to be discovered.

Together, in this exploration of gratitude,

Eric Osae-Twum

In this spirit of shared exploration and heartfelt thanksgiving,

Eric Osae-Twum: osaetwum@gmail.com

Acknowledgments

I thank God, the ever-present source of my strength and inspiration. This book is a testament to His boundless grace and enduring love.

I have been blessed with the support and guidance of many remarkable individuals, each contributing in unique and meaningful ways to make this devotional see the light of day. I am deeply grateful to my life and leadership coach, Reverend Kevin D. Cook, for his keen insight, steadfast dedication, and guidance, transforming my scattered thoughts and ideas into a coherent, resonant narrative. His patience and wisdom inspired me throughout this journey.

Thank you to my mother-in-law, Dinah Safo, for investing time in proofreading and offering insightful feedback. Your contributions have immeasurably enriched this work.

To my wife Stella and children, Abigail, Keith Daniel, Kevin Daniel, Keona-Dannette, Janric, Aljed, and Elvic, your understanding and love sustained me through countless hours of writing and revision, and your encouraging words comforted me.

And to you, the reader, for joining me in this exploration of faith and gratitude. May these words resonate with you as deeply as they have with me in writing them.

Table of Contents   **Page(s)**

Title Page………………………………………………………………………..1

Copyright Page………………………………………………………………….2

Dedication…………………………………………………………………………3

Foreword……………………………………………………………………….4-5

Preface………………………………………………………………………….6-7

Acknowledgement………………………………………………………………8

Table of Contents…………………………………………………………..9-13

Introduction: Embracing Gratitude……………………………….14-15

The Power of Gratitude: A counter Cultural Response…………..16

How to Navigate this Guide……………………………………………17-18

PART ONE: ~ ESSENCE OF GRATITUDE……………………………..19

Day 1: Embrace Every Moment……………………………………………20

Day 2: Roots of Gratitude………………………………………………….21

Day 3: Cultivating Thankfulness…………………………………………22

Day 4: Transformation Through Gratitude………………………….23

Day 5: Contentment and Appreciation………………………………..24

Day 6: The Ripple Effect of Appreciation……………………………25

Day 7: Worthiness and Gratitude……………………………………….26

Day 8: The Joy of Sharing Gratitude…………………………………..27

Day 9: Active Thankfulness………………………………………………..28

Day 10: Go and Sin No More……………………………………………..29

Day 11: Pathway to Joy……………………………………………………..30

Day 12: Perspective and Attitude..............................31

Day 13: Gift of the Present..............................32

Day 14: Finding Gratitude Amidst Trials..............................33

Day 15: Living with Awareness..............................34

Day 16: Privilege and Responsibility..............................35

Day 17: Love in the Now..............................36

Day 18: A Happy, Thankful Heart..............................37

Day 19: Uniting Through Gratitude..............................38

Day 20: Healing with Thankfulness..............................39

Day 21: Appreciating Life's Journey..............................40

Day 22: Daily Gifts..............................41

Day 23: Miracles in the Mundane..............................42

Day 24: Abundance and Appreciation..............................43

Day 25: Seeing Through God's Eyes..............................44

PART TWO: ~ GRATITUDE IN EVERY SEASON..............................45-46

Day 26: Gratefulness in All Things..............................47

Day 27: Trust Amid Trials..............................48

Day 28: Joy in Simplicity..............................49

Day 29: A Heart Filled with Thanks..............................50

Day 30: A Shift in Perspective..............................51

Day 31: Divine Gifts of Life..............................52

Day 32: Blessings and Thankfulness..............................53

Day 33: Life's Sustenance..............................54

Day 34: Wisdom in Contentment..................................55

Day 35: Life-Altering Blessings..................................56

Day 36: Excellence and Appreciation..................................57

Day 37: Gratitude as Courtesy..................................58

Day 38: Continual Thanksgiving..................................59

Day 39: Happiness for Others..................................60

Day 40: Memory of the Heart..................................61

Day 41: Strength Training the Heart..................................62

Day 42: Enrichment Through Thanks..................................63

Day 43: Unlocking Life's Fullness..................................64

Day 44: Gratitude's Alchemy..................................65

Day 45: Miraculous Turns..................................66

Day 46: Dance of Contentment..................................67

Day 47: Gratitude Through Life's Phases..................................68

Day 48: Faithful Thankfulness..................................69

PART THREE: ~ GRATITUDE AMIDST ADVERSITY..................................70-71

Day 49: Hardships as Divine Prep..................................72

Day 50: Simplicity in Thanks..................................73

Day 51: Treasures in Trials..................................74

Day 52: Guided Actions..................................75

Day 53: Humility and Thankfulness..................................76

Day 54: Foundations of Happiness..................................77

Day 55: Daily Joy..................................78

Day 56: Emotional Ebbs and Flows..79

Day 57: Prayer's Comfort..80

Day 58: Overcoming Fear..81

Day 59: Choice Above Circumstance..82

Day 60: Forgiveness and Gratitude..83

Day 61: Duty of Thanks..84

Day 62: Commandment of Success..85

Day 63: Infectious Gratefulness..86

Day 64: Adversity's Beauty..87

Day 65: Sign of Noble Souls..88

Day 66: Catalyst for Joy..89

Day 67: Life's Splendor..90

PART FOUR: FAITH AND TRUST IN DIVINE TIMING..91-92

Day 68: Gratitude for Impact..93

Day 69: Eternal Gratitude..94

Day 70: Seizing Opportunities..95

Day 71: Paths of Reverence..96

Day 72: Unlimited Thanks..97

Day 73: Cultivating a Thankful Heart..98

Day 74: Abundance in Thanks..99

Day 75: Gratitude at Work..100

Day 76: Fruits of Thankfulness..101

Day 77: Soulful Nurturing..102

Day 78: Appreciative Heart..103

Day 79: Unlocking Divine Blessings....................................104

Day 80: A Compass in the Storm.......................................105

Day 81: Consistent Devotion...106

Day 82: Balancing Aspirations..107

Day 83: New Beginnings..108

Day 84: Appreciating What You Have..................................109

Day 85: Simple Blessings...110

Day 86: Belief and Perseverance.......................................111

Day 87: Daily Intention...112

Day 88: Revealing Potential..113

Day 89: Mindfulness and Kindness....................................114

Day 90: Joy in Divine Timing...115

Conclusion: Embracing everlasting Gratitude: 116

Epilogue: Charting the path forward...................................117

Appendix: Daily Gratitude Practices: 118-119

Introduction

It was about 2:15 pm when my phone rang. My heart stopped. Why is my sister calling me? I asked myself. Her wailing voice said it all. My dearest mom had transitioned to heaven. How could that be? I spoke to her the previous day, and she was ok. Feelings of anger quickly filled me. I screamed and cried and hoped it was a mistake. I could not embrace reality. As I wallowed in my grief all afternoon, it suddenly hit me that Mom had lived an additional 40 years since my father passed away. I began to struggle with two opposing feelings: loss and gratitude. She was gone, and I would never see her again in her physical form. She had left a vacuum that would never be replaced. But she had single-handedly nurtured and raised us since my dad passed on in 1982 at the prime age of 40. As much as I wanted to sit in my pain and grief, I continuously experienced an unexplained sense of peace and gratitude. I was grateful that she had been my mom, raised me to become the man I am, and been here long enough to see and spend time with all her grandchildren.

It is challenging to feel grateful in today's rapid technological advancements, socio-political upheavals, and existential threats such as global health crises. Many feel disconnected, disillusioned, and overwhelmed by the relentless pace of news and the divisive nature of social media. However, there is no doubt that gratitude inspires hope in these turbulent times. Gratitude can be an active choice, a counterbalance to chaos, allowing us to see beyond the darkness and appreciate life's ephemeral light moments.

This 90-day devotional demonstrates how embracing gratitude can shift you from survival to thriving within the storm. It invites you to confront our world's harsh realities while seeking moments of grace and resilience.

The purpose of this book is twofold: 1. to call the people who read it to action, igniting inspiration and offering guidance. And 2. to touch the lives of even more people by directing the book sale profits to an exceptional course. Angels On Earth is a nonprofit organization in Ghana that sponsors children who have lost either one or both parents and, therefore, are unable to enjoy the full benefits of education and care. These children are offered full scholarships throughout their early years as they receive a Christ-centered education to build a solid foundation and shape their identity. The profits of the Culture of Gratitude book sale money will be used to support the mission of Angels On Earth to ensure that these disadvantaged children no longer have to deal with the pain of loss and the associated consequences that arise. You are helping us reach our goal of a hundred thousand copies sold and, in turn, helping hundreds of children in Ghana. Thank you for contributing to this world-changing legacy.

This book was written for you. I purposefully have not had it professionally edited because I wanted it to read as if I was having a personal conversation with you. If you are educated, that's great, but you don't need to feel as if you are book-smart before you develop a culture of gratitude. I have read many books over the years that were hard to read because the authors had great writers that made them look brilliant. I would rather have you get a lot in this book than have you set it aside and think this is not easy to comprehend. I hope you feel inspired and encouraged by the words on these pages. Join us on this voyage of understanding, reflection, and gratitude as we seek to comprehend and find beauty in our challenging times.

The Power of Gratitude: A Counter-Cultural Response

In a world that constantly highlights our deficiencies and desires, gratitude emerges as a powerful, counter-cultural act. It's a response that embraces the richness of the present moment despite challenges and promotes contentment, connection, and resilience. Let's examine some aspects of Gratitude.

1. **Resistance:** ~ Gratitude is resistance against societal norms that breeds dissatisfaction. It's an internal acknowledgment of life's inherent value, shifting focus from what we lack to what we have.
2. **Transformative Perspective:** ~ Gratitude can dramatically alter our perspective. Faced with the same challenges, a grateful person may see opportunities where others see obstacles. This perspective doesn't diminish pain but integrates it into life's broader fabric.
3. **Building Resilience:** ~ In a world of uncertainty, gratitude nurtures resilience. Acknowledging and appreciating what we have creates inner stability that withstands external turmoil.
4. **An Action:** ~ Far from passive, gratitude can inspire action. Appreciating the good can motivate us to extend kindness and generosity to others.
5. **A Daily Choice:** ~ Embracing gratitude requires intentionality. It's a commitment to focus on abundance, possibility, and hope, transforming from a periodic practice to a way of life.

In summary, cultivating gratitude offers a sanctuary from the relentless pursuit of "more." It's a conscious choice to find contentment and recognition of beauty in our world. As you engage with this guide, let gratitude lead you to a life of deeper fulfillment and joy.

How to Navigate This Guide

Welcome to your 90-day journey through the Culture of Gratitude. Here are some personalized steps to help you fully engage with this journey:

Embrace the Journey: Approach this guide with openness and patience. It's structured for 90 days, but feel free to move at your own pace, especially if a devotion strikes a deeper chord.

Daily Structure: Each day includes:

- A theme that sets the tone.
- A scripture and quote for context.
- A reflection for meditation.
- A prayer or gratitude moment for spiritual connection and
- An action Point to apply to the day's lesson.

Interactive Engagement: Mark resonating passages with bookmarks and highlights. These can become quick references for future reflection.

Adapt and Apply: The action points are designed to be adaptable. Tailor them to fit your life and challenge yourself to integrate these lessons meaningfully.

Share and Grow: Share your experiences with friends and family. Sharing can open new perspectives and deepen your journey.

Return and Rediscover: This guide remains a resource after 90 days. As gratitude grows and you change, revisiting the guide can offer new insights.

Patience on Tough Days: Some devotions may challenge you more than others. These days, remember that growth often comes from discomfort. Be gentle with yourself and stay open to the lessons these challenges bring.

Join Our Community: Finally, you'll find ways to connect and share your feedback. Your journey can inspire and support others.

In summary, let this guide be not just a 90-day journey but a life companion. It is designed to light up your path, challenge your perspectives, and deepen your gratitude experience. Here's to a journey of transformation and discovery!

PART ONE: ~ ESSENCE OF GRATITUDE

The essence of Gratitude begins by demystifying this deep emotion. Here, we delve into the origins and definitions of gratitude, weaving together scriptural insights, personal stories, and reflective explorations to uncover its multi-layered importance. Gratitude is more than a brief feeling; it is a mindset, a way of life that transforms our interactions and perspectives. We'll explore how different cultures and historical periods have embraced gratitude, providing a rich, global context to this universal virtue. This theoretical and convenient foundational knowledge offers tools to recognize, embrace, and cultivate gratitude daily. Prepare to embark on a journey that will enrich your understanding of gratitude, paving the way for a transformative practice that extends beyond these pages into the fabric of your existence. Let us dive in:

Day 1: ~ Embrace Every Moment:

"In happy moments, praise God. In difficult moments, seek God. In quiet moments, worship God. In painful moments, trust God. In every moment, thank God." ~ **Rick Warren.**

Scripture insight:

- **1 Thessalonians 5:16-18 (NIV):** ~ "Rejoice always, pray continually, give thanks in all circumstances; for this is God's will for you in Christ Jesus."

I AM GRATEFUL FOR THE FOLLOWING:

_____

_____

_____

WHAT WOULD MAKE TODAY GREAT?

_____

_____

_____

AFFIRMATIONS:

_____

_____

_____

HIGHLIGHTS:

_____

_____

_____

LESSONS:

_____

_____

_____

Day 2: ~ Roots of Gratitude

"Gratitude is not only the greatest of virtues but the parent of all the others." ~ **Marcus Tullius Cicero**

Scripture insight:

- **Colossians 3:17 (NIV)** ~ "And whatever you do, whether in word or deed, do it all in the name of the Lord Jesus, giving thanks to God the Father through him."

I AM GRATEFUL FOR THE FOLLOWING:

_____
_____
_____

WHAT WOULD MAKE TODAY GREAT?

_____
_____
_____

AFFIRMATIONS:

_____
_____
_____

HIGHLIGHTS:

_____
_____
_____

LESSONS:

_____
_____
_____

Day 3: ~ Cultivating Thankfulness

"Gratitude isn't just a feeling. It's an action. Expressing gratitude by writing in a journal, taking a photo, or shooting a video creates a lasting impression that can bring more gratitude into the world." ~ **Janice Kaplan**

Scripture Insight:

- **Psalm 100:4 (NIV):** ~ "Enter his gates with thanksgiving and his courts with praise; give thanks to him and praise his name."

I AM GRATEFUL FOR THE FOLLOWING:

_____

_____

_____

_____

WHAT WOULD MAKE TODAY GREAT?

_____

_____

_____

AFFIRMATIONS:

_____

_____

_____

HIGHLIGHTS:

_____

_____

_____

LESSONS:

_____

_____

_____

Day 4: ~ Transformation Through Gratitude

"Gratitude makes sense of our past, brings peace for today, and creates a vision for tomorrow." ~ **Melody Beattie**

Scripture insight:

- **Psalm 136:26 (NIV):** ~ "Give thanks to the God of heaven, for his steadfast love endures forever."

I AM GRATEFUL FOR THE FOLLOWING:

_____
_____
_____
_____

WHAT WOULD MAKE TODAY GREAT?

_____
_____
_____
_____

AFFIRMATIONS:

_____
_____
_____

HIGHLIGHTS:

_____
_____
_____

LESSONS:

_____
_____
_____

Day 5: ~ Contentment and Appreciation

"Gratitude turns what we have into enough." ~ **Aesop**

Scripture insight:

- **Philippians 4:11- 12 (NIV):** ~ "I am not saying this because I am in need, for I have learned to be content whatever the circumstances. I know what it is to be in need, and I know what it is to have plenty. I have learned the secret of being content in any and every situation, whether well fed or hungry, whether living in plenty or in want."

I AM GRATEFUL FOR THE FOLLOWING:

_____
_____
_____

WHAT WOULD MAKE TODAY GREAT?

_____
_____
_____

AFFIRMATIONS:

_____
_____
_____

HIGHLIGHTS:

_____
_____
_____

LESSONS:

_____
_____

Day 6: ~ The Ripple Effects of Appreciation

"Appreciation can make a day, even change a life. Your willingness to put it into words is all that is necessary." ~ **Margaret Cousins**

Scripture Insight:

- **1 Thessalonians 5:11 (NIV):** ~ "Therefore encourage one another and build each other up, just as you are doing."

I AM GRATEFUL FOR THE FOLLOWING:

_____
_____
_____
_____

WHAT WOULD MAKE TODAY GREAT?

_____
_____
_____

AFFIRMATIONS:

_____
_____
_____

HIGHLIGHTS:

_____
_____
_____

LESSONS:

_____
_____
_____

Day 7: ~ Worthiness and Gratitude

*"Strive to find things to be thankful for, and just look for the good in who you are." * ~ **Bethany Hamilton**

Scripture insight:

- **Ephesians 2:10 (NIV):** ~ "For we are God's handiwork, created in Christ Jesus to do good works, which God prepared in for us to do."

I AM GRATEFUL FOR FOLLOWING:

_____

_____

_____

_____

WHAT WOULD MAKE TODAY GREAT?

_____

_____

_____

AFFIRMATIONS:

_____

_____

_____

HIGHLIGHTS:

_____

_____

_____

LESSONS:

_____

_____

_____

Day 8: ~ The Joy of Sharing Gratitude.

"Silent gratitude isn't very much to anyone." ~ **Gertrude Stein**

Scripture insight:

- **Colossians 4:6 (NIV):** ~ "Let your conversation be always full of grace, seasoned with salt, so that you may know how to answer everyone."

I AM GRATEFUL FOR THE FOLLOWING:

_____
_____
_____
_____

WHAT WOULD MAKE TODAY GREAT?

_____
_____
_____
_____

AFFIRMATIONS:

_____
_____
_____

HIGHLIGHTS:

_____
_____
_____

LESSONS:

_____
_____
_____

Day 9: ~ Active Thankfulness.

"One can never pay in gratitude; one can only pay 'in kind' somewhere else in life." ~ **Anne Morrow Lindbergh**.

Scripture insight:

- **Luke 6:38 (NIV):** ~ "Give, and it will be given to you. A good measure, pressed down, shaken together, and running over, will be poured into your lap. For with the measure you use, it will be measured to you."

I AM GRATEFUL FOR THE FOLLOWING:

_____
_____
_____

WHAT WOULD MAKE TODAY GREAT?

_____
_____
_____

AFFIRMATIONS:

_____
_____
_____

HIGHLIGHTS:

_____
_____
_____

LESSONS:

_____
_____
_____

Day 10: ~ Go and Sin No More

"Thanksgiving is a special virtue. But ingratitude is opposed to Thanksgiving. Therefore, ingratitude is a special sin." ~ **Thomas Aquinas.**

Scripture insight:

- **Romans 1:21 (NIV):** ~ "For although they knew God, they neither glorified him as God nor gave thanks to him, but their thinking became futile, and their foolish hearts were darkened."

I AM GRATEFUL FOR THE FOLLOWING:

_____
_____
_____
_____

WHAT WOULD MAKE TODAY GREAT?

_____
_____
_____

AFFIRMATIONS:

_____
_____
_____

HIGHLIGHTS:

_____
_____
_____

LESSONS:

_____
_____
_____

Day 11: ~ Pathway to Joy

"Thankfulness is the quickest path to joy." ~ **Jefferson Bethke**

Scripture insight:

- **1 Thessalonians 5:16-18 (NIV):** ~ Rejoice always, pray continually, give thanks in all circumstances; for this is God's will for you in Christ Jesus.

I AM GRATEFUL FOR THE FOLLOWING:

_____

_____

_____

_____

WHAT WOULD MAKE TODAY GREAT?

_____

_____

_____

_____

AFFIRMATIONS:

_____

_____

_____

HIGHLIGHTS:

_____

_____

_____

LESSONS:

_____

_____

_____

Day 12: ~ Perspective and Attitude

"Gratitude and attitude are not challenges; they are choices." ~ **Robert Braathe**

Scripture insight:

- **Philippians 2:5 (NIV):** ~ "In your relationships with one another, have the same mindset as Christ Jesus."

I AM GRATEFUL FOR THE FOLLOWING:

_____

_____

_____

_____

WHAT WOULD MAKE TODAY GREAT?

_____

_____

_____

_____

AFFIRMATIONS:

_____

_____

_____

HIGHLIGHTS:

_____

_____

_____

LESSONS:

_____

_____

_____

Day 13: ~ The Gift of the Present

"Reflect upon your present blessings, of which every man has plenty; not on your past misfortunes, of which all men have some." ~ **Charles Dickens**.

Scripture insight:

- **Psalm 34:8 (NIV):** ~ "Taste and see that the Lord is good; blessed is the one who takes refuge in him."

I AM GRATEFUL FOR THE FOLLOWING:

_____

_____

_____

_____

WHAT WOULD MAKE TODAY GREAT?

_____

_____

_____

_____

AFFIRMATIONS:

_____

_____

_____

HIGHLIGHTS:

_____

_____

_____

LESSONS:

_____

_____

_____

Day 14: ~ Finding Gratitude Amidst Trials

"When you arise in the morning, think of what a precious privilege it is to be alive - to breathe, to think, to enjoy, to love." ~ **Marcus Aurelius**.

Scripture insight:

- **James 1:2-4 (NIV)**: ~ "Consider it pure joy, my brothers and sisters, whenever you face trials of many kinds, because you know that the testing of your faith produces perseverance."

I AM GRATEFUL FOR THE FOLLOWING:

_____
_____
_____
_____

WHAT WOULD MAKE TODAY GREAT?

_____
_____
_____

AFFIRMATIONS:

_____
_____
_____

HIGHLIGHTS:

_____
_____
_____

LESSONS:

_____
_____
_____

Day 15: ~ Living with Awareness

"We can only be said to be alive in those moments when our hearts are conscious of our treasures." ~ **Thornton Wilder**

Scripture insight:

- **Psalm 118:24 (NIV):** ~ "This is the day the LORD has made; let us rejoice and be glad in it."

I AM GRATEFUL FOR THE FOLLOWING:

_____
_____
_____
_____

WHAT WOULD MAKE TODAY GREAT?

_____
_____
_____
_____

AFFIRMATIONS:

_____
_____
_____

HIGHLIGHTS:

_____
_____
_____

LESSONS:

_____
_____
_____

Day 16: ~ Privilege and Responsibility

"What separates privilege from entitlement is gratitude." ~ **Brené Brown**

Scripture insight:

- **1 Corinthians 4:7 (NIV)**: ~ "For who makes you different from anyone else? What do you have that you did not receive? And if you did receive it, why do you boast as though you did not?"

I AM GRATEFUL FOR THE FOLLOWING:

_____
_____
_____
_____

WHAT WOULD MAKE TODAY GREAT?

_____
_____
_____
_____

AFFIRMATIONS:

_____
_____
_____

HIGHLIGHTS:

_____
_____
_____

LESSONS:

_____
_____
_____

Day 17: ~ Love in the Now

"Gratitude looks to the Past and love to the Present; fear, avarice, lust, and ambition look ahead." ~ **C.S. Lewis.**

Scripture insight:

- **Psalm 118:24 (NIV):** ~ "This is the day the Lord has made; let us rejoice and be glad in it."

I AM GRATEFUL FOR THE FOLLOWING:

_____
_____
_____
_____

WHAT WOULD MAKE TODAY GREAT?

_____
_____
_____
_____

AFFIRMATIONS:

_____
_____
_____

HIGHLIGHTS:

_____
_____
_____

LESSONS:

_____
_____
_____

Day 18: ~ A Happy Thankful Heart

"The heart that gives thanks is a happy one, for we cannot feel thankful and unhappy at the same time." ~ **Douglas Wood.**

Scripture insight:

- **Psalm 28:7 (NIV):** ~ "The Lord is my strength and my shield; my heart trusts in him, and he helps me. My heart leaps for joy, and with my song, I praise him."

I AM GRATEFUL FOR THE FOLLOWING:

_____
_____
_____
_____

WHAT WOULD MAKE TODAY GREAT?

_____
_____
_____

AFFIRMATIONS:

_____
_____
_____

HIGHLIGHTS:

_____
_____
_____

LESSONS:

_____
_____
_____

Day 19: ~ Uniting Through Gratitude

"There is only one thing that can form a bond between men, and that is gratitude... we cannot give someone else greater power over us than we have ourselves." ~ **Montesquieu.**

Scripture insight:

- **Psalm 133:1 (NIV):** ~ "How good and pleasant it is when God's people live together in unity!"

I AM GRATEFUL FOR THE FOLLOWING:

_____

_____

_____

_____

WHAT WOULD MAKE TODAY GREAT?

_____

_____

_____

AFFIRMATIONS:

_____

_____

_____

HIGHLIGHTS:

_____

_____

_____

LESSONS:

_____

_____

_____

Day 20: ~ Healing with Thankfulness

"Gratitude is the healthiest of all human emotions. The more you express gratitude for what you have, the more likely you will have even more to express gratitude for." ~ **Zig Ziglar**

Scripture insight:

- **Psalm 107:1 (NIV):** ~ "Give thanks to the Lord, for he is good; his love endures forever."

I AM GRATEFUL FOR THE FOLLOWING:

_____

_____

_____

_____

WHAT WOULD MAKE TODAY GREAT?

_____

_____

_____

AFFIRMATIONS:

_____

_____

_____

HIGHLIGHTS:

_____

_____

_____

LESSONS:

_____

_____

_____

Day 21: ~ Appreciating Life's Journey

"Things turn out best for people who make the best of how things turn out." ~ **John Wooden**

Scripture insight:

- **Romans 8:28 (NIV):** ~ "And we know that in all things God works for the good of those who love him, who have been called according to his purpose."

I AM GRATEFUL FOR THE FOLLOWING:

_____

_____

_____

_____

WHAT WOULD MAKE TODAY GREAT?

_____

_____

_____

AFFIRMATIONS:

_____

_____

_____

HIGHLIGHTS:

_____

_____

_____

LESSONS:

_____

_____

_____

Day 22: ~ Daily Gifts

"A grateful heart sees each day as a gift. Thankful people focus less on what they lack and more on the privileges they have." ~ **Max Lucado.**

Scripture insight:

- **Psalm 118:24 (NIV):** ~ "This is the day that the Lord has made; let us rejoice and be glad in it."

I AM GRATEFUL FOR THE FOLLOWING:

_____
_____
_____
_____

WHAT WOULD MAKE TODAY GREAT?

_____
_____
_____
_____

AFFIRMATIONS:

_____
_____
_____

HIGHLIGHTS:

_____
_____
_____

LESSONS:

_____
_____
_____

Day 23: ~ Miracles in the Mundane

"There are only two ways to live your life. One is as though nothing is a miracle. The other is as though everything is a miracle." ~ **Albert Einstein**

Scripture insight:

- **Psalm 19:1 (NIV):** ~ "The heavens declare the glory of God; the skies proclaim the work of his hands."

I AM GRATEFUL FOR THE FOLLOWING:

_____
_____
_____
_____

WHAT WOULD MAKE TODAY GREAT?

_____
_____
_____
_____

AFFIRMATIONS:

_____
_____
_____

HIGHLIGHTS:

_____
_____
_____

LESSONS:

_____
_____
_____

Day 24: ~ Abundance and Appreciation

"If you don't appreciate what you have, you may as well not have it." ~
Rosalene Glickman

Scripture insight:

- **Hebrews 13:5 (NIV):** ~ "Keep your lives free from the love of money and be content with what you have, because God has said, never will I leave you; never will I forsake you."

I AM GRATEFUL FOR THE FOLLOWING:

_____
_____
_____
_____

WHAT WOULD MAKE TODAY GREAT?

_____
_____
_____

AFFIRMATIONS:

_____
_____
_____

HIGHLIGHTS:

_____
_____
_____

LESSONS:

_____
_____
_____

Day 25: ~ Seeing Through God's Eyes

"People only see what they are prepared to see. If you look for what is good and what you can be grateful for, you will find it everywhere." ~ **Ralph Waldo Emerson**

Scripture insight:

- **Matthew 7:7 (NIV):** ~ "Ask and it will be given to you; seek, and you will find; knock, and the door will be opened to you. "

I AM GRATEFUL FOR THE FOLLOWING:

_____
_____
_____
_____

WHAT WOULD MAKE TODAY GREAT?

_____
_____
_____

AFFIRMATIONS:

_____
_____
_____

HIGHLIGHTS:

_____
_____
_____

LESSONS:

_____
_____
_____

PART TWO: ~ GRATITUDE IN EVERY SEASON:

Our Christian call to gratitude in all circumstances is a vital and fundamental aspect of our faith and the broader human experience. Gratitude, in this context, is not a feeling of thankfulness when things go well but a way of life and a spiritual practice that transcends circumstances. Let's see how gratitude as a way of life can impact us:

1. **Biblical Foundations:** Gratitude is deeply rooted in Christian theology. The Bible contains many references to giving thanks in all circumstances. For example, 1 Thessalonians 5:18 states, "Give thanks in all circumstances; for this is the will of God in Christ Jesus for you." The Christian call to gratitude is God's will for us as believers.

2. **Trust in Divine Providence:** God is the ultimate source of all blessings; even in challenging times, there is a reason for gratitude. We are therefore encouraged to trust in God's providence, believing that everything that happens, positive or negative, is part of a larger divine plan. This way, we will be grounded in faith and our calling.

3. **Spiritual Growth:** The practice of gratitude enhances our spiritual growth and transformation. It helps focus on the blessings received rather than the lack, encouraging contentment and a more sincere faith.

4. **Compassion and Generosity:** Gratitude can inspire acts of kindness and generosity. Christians are called to receive and give, sharing their blessings with those in need. Gratitude motivates believers to be instruments of God's love and provision.

5. **Resilience and Endurance:** The Christian call to gratitude always emphasizes resilience and endurance in trials. By finding reasons to be thankful even during difficult times, believers can find strength to persevere and grow spiritually.

6. **Community and Worship:** Gratitude is often expressed in communal worship and prayer. Christian communities come together to give thanks for the blessings they've received, encouraging unity and shared faith.

7. **Humility:** Gratitude nurtures humility by reminding believers that their blessings are gifts from God, not solely the result of their efforts. This humility helps individuals avoid arrogance and pride.
8. **Eternal Perspective:** Christianity teaches that life on Earth is temporary, and the goal is eternal life with God. Gratitude in all circumstances helps believers maintain an eternal perspective, recognizing that the challenges of this world are temporary compared to the glory that awaits in the afterlife.
9. **Witness to the World:** Practicing gratitude in all circumstances can be a powerful witness to others. When Christians maintain a thankful spirit even in the face of adversity, it can inspire curiosity and interest in their faith and way of life.

In summary, the human and Christian call to gratitude always is a deeply spiritual and transformative practice. It encourages believers to see every moment, whether joyful or challenging, as an opportunity to express thanksgiving and trust in God's plan. Gratitude strengthens our relationship with God and leads to a more compassionate, generous, and resilient life. It serves as a reminder that there is always a reason to give thanks, regardless of the circumstances.

Day 26: ~ Gratefulness in All Things

"We can always find something to be thankful for, and there may be reasons why we ought to be thankful for even those dispensations which appear dark and frowning." ~ **Albert Barnes**

Scripture insight:

- **Romans 8:28 (NIV):** ~ "And we know that in all things God works for the good of those who love him, who have been called according to his purpose."

I AM GRATEFUL FOR THE FOLLOWING:

_____
_____
_____

WHAT WOULD MAKE TODAY GREAT?

_____
_____
_____

AFFIRMATIONS:

_____
_____
_____

HIGHLIGHTS:

_____
_____
_____

LESSONS:

_____
_____
_____

Day 27: ~ Trust amid Trials

"I have learned to kiss the wave that throws me against the Rock of Ages."
~ **Charles Spurgeon**.

Scripture insight:

- **James 1:2-3 (NIV):** ~ "Consider it pure joy, my brothers and sisters, whenever you face trials of many kinds, because you know that the testing of your faith produces perseverance."

I AM GRATEFUL FOR THE FOLLOWING:

_____
_____
_____
_____

WHAT WOULD MAKE TODAY GREAT?

_____
_____
_____

AFFIRMATIONS:

_____
_____
_____

HIGHLIGHTS:

_____
_____
_____

LESSONS:

_____
_____
_____

Day 28: ~ Joy in Simplicity

"Enjoy the little things, for one day you may look back and realize they were the big things." ~ **Robert Brault**

Scripture insight:

- **Luke 16:10 (NIV)**: ~ "Whoever can be trusted with very little can also be trusted with much, and whoever is dishonest with very little will also be dishonest with much."

I AM GRATEFUL FOR THE FOLLOWING:

_____
_____
_____

WHAT WOULD MAKE TODAY GREAT?

_____
_____
_____

AFFIRMATIONS:

_____
_____
_____

HIGHLIGHTS:

_____
_____
_____

LESSONS:

_____
_____
_____

Day 29: ~ A Heart Filled with Thanks

"O Lord that lends me life, lend me a heart replete with thankfulness." ~ **William Shakespeare**.

Scripture insight:

- **Psalm 100:4 (NIV)**: ~ "Enter his gates with thanksgiving and his courts with praise; give thanks to him and praise his name."

I AM GRATEFUL FOR THE FOLLOWING:

_____
_____
_____
_____

WHAT WOULD MAKE TODAY GREAT?

_____
_____
_____
_____

AFFIRMATIONS:

_____
_____
_____

HIGHLIGHTS:

_____
_____
_____

LESSONS:

_____
_____
_____

Day 30: ~ A Shift in Perspective

"When it comes to life, the critical thing is whether you take things for granted or take them with gratitude." — **G.K. Chesterton**

Scripture insight:

- **1 Thessalonians 5:18 (NIV):** ~ "Give thanks in all circumstances; for this is God's will for you in Christ Jesus."

I AM GRATEFUL FOR THE FOLLOWING:

_____

_____

_____

_____

WHAT WOULD MAKE TODAY GREAT?

_____

_____

_____

AFFIRMATIONS:

_____

_____

_____

_____

HIGHLIGHTS:

_____

_____

_____

LESSONS:

_____

_____

_____

Day 31: ~ Divine Gifts of Life

"Gratitude is the ability to experience life as a gift. It liberates us from the prison of self-preoccupation." ~ **John Ortberg**

Scripture insight:

- **Colossians 3:2 (NIV):** ~ "Set your minds on things above, not on earthly things."

I AM GRATEFUL FOR THE FOLLOWING:

_____
_____
_____
_____

WHAT WOULD MAKE TODAY GREAT?

_____
_____
_____
_____

AFFIRMATIONS:

_____
_____
_____

HIGHLIGHTS:

_____
_____
_____

LESSONS:

_____
_____
_____

Day 32: ~ Blessings and Thankfulness

"The unthankful heart discovers no mercies, but the thankful heart will find, in every hour, some heavenly blessings." ~ **Henry Ward Beecher**.

Scripture insight:

- **James 1:17 (NIV):** ~ "Every good and perfect gift is from above, coming down from the Father of the heavenly lights, who does not change like shifting shadows."

I AM GRATEFUL FOR THE FOLLOWING:

_____
_____
_____
_____

WHAT WOULD MAKE TODAY GREAT?

_____
_____
_____

AFFIRMATIONS:

_____
_____
_____

HIGHLIGHTS:

_____
_____
_____

LESSONS:

_____
_____
_____

Day 33: ~ Life's Sustenance

"Wear gratitude like a cloak, and it will feed every corner of your life." ~ **Rumi**.

Scripture insight:

- **Colossians 3:17 (NIV):** ~ "And whatever you do, whether in word or deed, do it all in the name of the Lord Jesus, giving thanks to God the Father through him."

I AM GRATEFUL FOR THE FOLLOWING:

_____
_____
_____
_____

WHAT WOULD MAKE TODAY GREAT?

_____
_____
_____

AFFIRMATIONS:

_____
_____
_____

HIGHLIGHTS:

_____
_____
_____

LESSONS:

_____
_____
_____

Day 34: ~ Wisdom in Contentment

*"He is a wise man who does not grieve for the things which he has not but rejoices for those which he has." ~***Epictetus.**

Scripture insight:

- **1 Timothy 6:6 (NIV):** ~ "But godliness with contentment is great gain."

I AM GRATEFUL FOR THE FOLLOWING:

_____
_____
_____
_____

WHAT WOULD MAKE TODAY GREAT?

_____
_____
_____
_____

AFFIRMATIONS:

_____
_____
_____

HIGHLIGHTS:

_____
_____
_____

LESSONS:

_____
_____
_____

Day 35: ~ Life-Altering Blessings

"When I started counting my blessings, my whole life turned around." ~ **Willie Nelson**

Scripture insight:

- **Psalm 28:7 (NIV):** ~ "The Lord is my strength and my shield; my heart trusts in him, and he helps me. My heart leaps for joy, and with my song I praise him."

I AM GRATEFUL FOR THE FOLLOWING:

_____
_____
_____
_____

WHAT WOULD MAKE TODAY GREAT?

_____
_____
_____

AFFIRMATIONS:

_____
_____
_____

HIGHLIGHTS:

_____
_____
_____

LESSONS:

_____
_____
_____

Day 36: ~ Excellence and Appreciation

"Appreciation is a wonderful thing. It makes what is excellent in others belong to us as well." ~ **Voltaire**.

Scripture insight:

- **Philippians 2:3-4 (NIV):** ~ "Do nothing out of selfish ambition or vain conceit. Rather, in humility, value others above yourselves, not looking to your interests but each of you to the interests of the others."

I AM GRATEFUL FOR THE FOLLOWING:

_____
_____
_____

WHAT WOULD MAKE TODAY GREAT?

_____
_____
_____

AFFIRMATIONS:

_____
_____
_____

HIGHLIGHTS:

_____
_____
_____

LESSONS:

_____
_____
_____

Day 37: ~ Gratitude as Courtesy

"Gratitude is the most exquisite form of courtesy." ~ **Jacques Maritain**

Scripture insight:

- **Colossians 3:12 (NIV):** ~ "Therefore, as God's chosen people, holy and dearly loved, clothe yourselves with compassion, kindness, humility, gentleness, and patience."

I AM GRATEFUL FOR THE FOLLOWING:

_____

_____

_____

_____

WHAT WOULD MAKE TODAY GREAT?

_____

_____

_____

_____

AFFIRMATIONS:

_____

_____

_____

HIGHLIGHTS:

_____

_____

_____

LESSONS:

_____

_____

_____

Day 38: ~ Continual Thanksgiving:

"Cultivate the habit of being grateful for every good thing that comes to you and to give thanks continuously. And because all things have contributed to your advancement, you should include all things in your gratitude." ~ **Ralph Waldo Emerson**.

Scripture insight:

- **1 Thessalonians 5:18 (NIV):** ~ "Give thanks in all circumstances; for this is God's will for you in Christ Jesus."

I AM GRATEFUL FOR THE FOLLOWING:

_____
_____
_____

WHAT WOULD MAKE TODAY GREAT?

_____
_____
_____

AFFIRMATIONS:

_____
_____

HIGHLIGHTS:

_____
_____
_____

LESSONS:

_____
_____
_____

Day 39: ~ Happiness for Others

"Let us be grateful to people who make us happy; they are the charming gardeners who make our souls blossom." ~ **Marcel Proust**

Scripture insight:

- **Proverbs 17:17 (NIV):** ~ "A friend loves at all times, and a brother is born for adversity."

I AM GRATEFUL FOR THE FOLLOWING:

_____
_____
_____
_____

WHAT WOULD MAKE TODAY GREAT?

_____
_____
_____
_____

AFFIRMATIONS:

_____
_____
_____

HIGHLIGHTS:

_____
_____
_____

LESSONS:

_____
_____
_____

Day 40: ~ Gratitude as the Memory of the Heart

"Gratitude is the memory of the heart." ~ **Jean Baptiste Massieu**

Scripture insight :

- **Psalm 103:2 (NIV):** ~ "Bless the Lord, O my soul, and forget not all his benefits."

I AM GRATEFUL FOR THE FOLLOWING:

_____

_____

_____

_____

_____

WHAT WOULD MAKE TODAY GREAT?

_____

_____

_____

_____

AFFIRMATIONS:

_____

_____

_____

HIGHLIGHTS:

_____

_____

_____

LESSONS:

_____

_____

_____

Day 41: ~ Strength Training the Heart

"Being thankful is not always experienced as a natural state of existence; we must work at it, akin to a type of strength training for the heart." ~ **Larissa Gomez**.

Scripture insight:

- **Colossians 3:17 (NIV):** ~ "And whatever you do, whether in word or deed, do it all in the name of the Lord Jesus, giving thanks to God the Father through him."

I AM GRATEFUL FOR THE FOLLOWING:

_____
_____
_____

WHAT WOULD MAKE TODAY GREAT?

_____
_____
_____

AFFIRMATIONS:

_____
_____
_____

HIGHLIGHTS:

_____
_____
_____

LESSONS:

_____
_____
_____

Day 42: ~ Enrichment Through Thanks

"Gratitude unlocks the fullness of life. It turns what we have into enough and more. It turns denial into acceptance, chaos into order, confusion into clarity, problems into gifts, failures into success, the unexpected into perfect timing, and mistakes into important events." ~ **Melody Beattie**.

Scripture insight:

- **Romans 8:28 (NIV):** ~ "And we know that in all things God works for the good of those who love him, who have been called according to his purpose."

I AM GRATEFUL FOR THE FOLLOWING:

_____
_____
_____

WHAT WOULD MAKE TODAY GREAT?

_____
_____
_____

AFFIRMATIONS:

_____
_____
_____

HIGHLIGHTS:

_____
_____
_____

LESSONS:

_____
_____

Day 43: ~ Unlocking Life's Fullness:

"The real gift of gratitude is that the more grateful you are, the more present you become." ~ **Robert Holden**

Scripture insight:

- **1 Thessalonians 5:16-18 (NIV):** - "Rejoice always, pray continually, give thanks in all circumstances; for this is God's will for you in Christ Jesus."

I AM GRATEFUL FOR THE FOLLOWING:

_____

_____

_____

_____

WHAT WOULD MAKE TODAY GREAT?

_____

_____

_____

AFFIRMATIONS:

_____

_____

_____

HIGHLIGHTS:

_____

_____

_____

LESSONS:

_____

_____

_____

Day 44: ~ Gratitude's Alchemy

"Gratitude can transform common days into Thanksgiving, turn routine jobs into joy, and change ordinary opportunities into blessings." ~ **William Arthur Ward.**

Scripture insight:

- **1 Thessalonians 5:18 (NIV):** ~ "Give thanks in all circumstances; for this is the will of God in Christ Jesus for you."

I AM GRATEFUL FOR THE FOLLOWING:

_____

_____

_____

_____

WHAT WOULD MAKE TODAY GREAT?

_____

_____

_____

AFFIRMATIONS:

_____

_____

_____

HIGHLIGHTS:

_____

_____

_____

LESSONS:

_____

_____

_____

Day 45: ~ Miraculous Turns

"Gratitude also opens your eyes to the limitless potential of the universe, while dissatisfaction closes your eyes to it." ~ **Stephen Richards**

Scripture Insight:

- **Psalm 100:4 (NIV):** ~ "Enter his gates with thanksgiving and his courts with praise; give thanks to him and praise his name."

I AM GRATEFUL FOR THE FOLLOWING:

_____

_____

_____

_____

WHAT WOULD MAKE TODAY GREAT?

_____

_____

_____

_____

AFFIRMATIONS:

_____

_____

_____

HIGHLIGHTS:

_____

_____

_____

LESSONS:

_____

_____

_____

Day 46: ~ Dance of Contentment

"If a fellow isn't thankful for what he's got, he isn't likely to be thankful for what he's going to get." ~ **Frank A. Clark**

Scripture insight:

- **Philippians 4:11-12 (NIV):** ~ "I have learned to be content whatever the circumstances... I have learned the secret of being content in every situation."

I AM GRATEFUL FOR THE FOLLOWING:

_____

_____

_____

_____

WHAT WOULD MAKE TODAY GREAT?

_____

_____

_____

AFFIRMATIONS:

_____

_____

_____

HIGHLIGHTS:

_____

_____

_____

LESSONS:

_____

_____

_____

Day 47: ~ Gratitude Through Life's Phases

"Be thankful for everything that happens in your life; it's all an experience." ~ **Roy T. Bennett**.

Scripture insight:

- **Ecclesiastes 3:1 (NIV):** ~ "There is a time for everything and a season for every activity under the heavens."

I AM GRATEFUL FOR THE FOLLOWING:

_____
_____
_____
_____

WHAT WOULD MAKE TODAY GREAT?

_____
_____
_____
_____

AFFIRMATIONS:

_____
_____
_____

HIGHLIGHTS:

_____
_____
_____

LESSONS:

_____
_____
_____

Day 48: ~ Faithful Thankfulness

"Thankfulness is not a reaction to something we're happy about; it's a belief that everything God does is for our good." ~ **Joyce Meyer**.

Scripture insight:

- **Psalm 34:8 (NIV):** ~ "Taste and see that the Lord is good; blessed is the one who takes refuge in him."

I AM GRATEFUL FOR THE FOLLOWING:

_____
_____
_____
_____

WHAT WOULD MAKE TODAY GREAT?

_____
_____
_____

AFFIRMATIONS:

_____
_____
_____
_____

HIGHLIGHTS:

_____
_____
_____

LESSONS:

_____
_____
_____

PART THREE: GRATITUDE AMIDST ADVERSITY

The notion of finding gratitude in adversity is deep. It inspires us to unearth avenues for development and perseverance even amidst challenges. It indicates a paradigm shift, encouraging us to discern the invaluable lessons embedded within hardships. Let's look at some of the facets of gratitude amid struggle and the prospects they unveil:

1. **Fortitude and Resilience:** In the face of adversity, the essence of one's resilience shines through. Embracing gratitude allows a deeper introspection, revealing innate capabilities and the prowess to surmount challenges.
2. **A Renewed Outlook:** Hard times often refine our worldview. We can direct our focus through gratitude, gravitating toward life's quintessential elements: cherishing the invaluable and frequently overlooked moments.
3. **Wisdom in Struggle:** Adversity is life's seasoned tutor. With gratitude, we unearth the knowledge of challenges and, thus, cultivate a more enlightened self.
4. **Empathy's Birthplace:** Tribulations nurture empathy. Gratitude amidst such times awakens an innate drive to uplift others, weaving harmony into community and kinship.
5. **Mentality of Tenacity:** Gratitude interlinks closely with tenacity. Instead of meditating on misfortunes, one can empower themselves by anchoring to inherent strengths and available support.
6. **Valuing the Pillars:** Tough times spotlight our pillars of support. Gratitude recognizes and amplifies appreciation for those unwavering figures, reinforcing trust and camaraderie.
7. **Molding Character:** Adversity is a crucible for character. We acknowledge the opportunity to refine and exhibit virtues like grit, courage, and ethics through gratitude.
8. **Nurturing Robust Coping Mechanisms:** Embodying gratitude in strife often births practical coping tools. Delving into practices such as mindfulness or seeking guidance promotes emotional equilibrium.

9. **Savoring Triumphs:** Conquering adversity bestows empowerment. Gratitude cherishes these victories, acknowledging the indomitable spirit within.

10. **Laying Future Cornerstones:** Adversity paradoxically often architects subsequent prosperity. Gratitude enhances an optimistic forward gaze, encouraging that current tribulations will pave the way for a brighter tomorrow.

In essence, gratitude amidst adversity reveals hidden pathways of development and resilience. It nudges us to unearth joy despite adversities and, because of them, transform challenges into a wellspring of fulfillment.

Day 49: ~ Hardships as Divine Preparation.

"Hardships often prepare ordinary people for an extraordinary destiny." ~ **C.S. Lewis**.

Scripture insight:

- **James 1:2-4 (NIV):** ~ "Consider it pure joy, my brothers and sisters, whenever you face trials of many kinds, because you know that the testing of your faith produces perseverance. Let perseverance finish its work so you may be mature and complete, not lacking anything."

I AM GRATEFUL FOR THE FOLLOWING:

_____

_____

_____

WHAT WOULD MAKE TODAY GREAT?

_____

_____

_____

AFFIRMATIONS:

_____

_____

_____

HIGHLIGHTS:

_____

_____

_____

LESSONS

_____

_____

Day 50: ~ Simplicity in Thanks

"If the only prayer you said was thank you, that would be enough." ~ **Meister Eckhart**

Scripture insight:

- **1 Thessalonians 5:16-18 (NIV):** ~ "Rejoice always, pray continually, give thanks in all circumstances; for this is God's will for you in Christ Jesus."

I AM GRATEFUL FOR THE FOLLOWING:

_____
_____
_____
_____

WHAT WOULD MAKE TODAY GREAT?

_____
_____
_____

AFFIRMATIONS:

_____
_____
_____

HIGHLIGHTS:

_____
_____
_____

LESSONS

_____
_____
_____

Day 51: ~ Treasures in Trials

"Sweet are the uses of adversity, which, like the toad, ugly and venomous, wears yet a precious jewel in his head." ~ **William Shakespeare**.

Scripture insight:

- **Hebrews 12:2 (NIV):** ~ "Fixing our eyes on Jesus, the pioneer and perfecter of faith. For the joy set before him, he endured the cross, scorning its shame, and sat down at the right hand of the throne of God."

I AM GRATEFUL FOR THE FOLLOWING:

_____
_____
_____

WHAT WOULD MAKE TODAY GREAT?

_____
_____
_____

AFFIRMATIONS:

_____
_____
_____

HIGHLIGHTS:

_____
_____
_____

LESSONS:

_____
_____
_____

Day 52: ~ Guided Actions.

"Everything we do should be a result of our gratitude for what God has done for us." ~ **Lauryn Hill**.

Scripture insight:

- **Colossians 3:17 (NIV):** ~ "And whatever you do, whether in word or deed, do it all in the name of the Lord Jesus, giving thanks to God the Father through him."

I AM GRATEFUL FOR THE FOLLOWING:

_____
_____
_____
_____

WHAT WOULD MAKE TODAY GREAT?

_____
_____
_____

AFFIRMATIONS:

_____
_____
_____

HIGHLIGHTS:

_____
_____
_____

LESSONS:

_____
_____
_____

Day 53: ~ Humility and Thankfulness

"I think gratitude is a big thing. It puts you in a place where you're humble." ~ **Andra Day**

Scripture insight:

- **James 4:10 (NIV):** ~ "Humble yourselves before the Lord, and he will lift you up."

I AM GRATEFUL FOR THE FOLLOWING:

_____

_____

_____

_____

WHAT WOULD MAKE TODAY GREAT?

_____

_____

_____

_____

AFFIRMATIONS:

_____

_____

_____

HIGHLIGHTS:

_____

_____

_____

LESSONS:

_____

_____

_____

Day 54: ~ Foundations of Happiness

"Of all the characteristics needed for a happy and morally decent life, none surpasses gratitude. Grateful people are happier, and grateful people are more morally decent." ~ **Dennis Prager**.

Scripture insight:

- **Colossians 3:15 (NIV):** ~ "Let the peace of Christ rule in your hearts, since as members of one body you were called to peace. And be thankful."

I AM GRATEFUL FOR THE FOLLOWING:

_____

_____

_____

_____

WHAT WOULD MAKE TODAY GREAT?

_____

_____

_____

AFFIRMATIONS:

_____

_____

_____

HIGHLIGHTS:

_____

_____

_____

LESSONS:

_____

_____

Day 55: ~ Daily Joy

"If you want to feel happier, start by incorporating a small dose of gratitude into your daily habit, whether it is on your commute, during a break, at a meal, or before you go to bed - it all adds up and can be very valuable to your health and well-being. You can also use it to inspire others." ~ **Joshua Rosenthal**

Scripture insight:

- **Psalm 118:24 (NIV):** ~ "This is the day the Lord has made; let us rejoice and be glad in it."

I AM GRATEFUL FOR THE FOLLOWING:

_____
_____
_____

WHAT WOULD MAKE TODAY GREAT?

_____
_____
_____

AFFIRMATIONS:

_____
_____
_____

HIGHLIGHTS:

_____
_____
_____

LESSONS:

_____
_____

Day 56: ~ Emotional Declines and Flows

"When we focus on our gratitude, the tide of disappointment goes out and the tide of love rushes in." ~ **Kristin Armstrong**.

Scripture insight:

- **1 Peter 4:8 (NIV):** ~ "Above all, love each other deeply, because love covers over a multitude of sins."

I AM GRATEFUL FOR THE FOLLOWING:

_____
_____
_____
_____

WHAT WOULD MAKE TODAY GREAT?

_____
_____
_____
_____

AFFIRMATIONS:

_____
_____
_____

HIGHLIGHTS:

_____
_____
_____

LESSONS:

_____
_____
_____

Day 57: ~ Prayer's Comfort

"When night falls and we draw the curtains close, let gratitude be the soft pillow upon which we rest our heads and hearts in prayer." ~ **Maya Angelou**

Scripture insight:

- **Colossians 4:2 (NIV):** ~ "Devote yourselves to prayer, being watchful and thankful."

I AM GRATEFUL FOR THE FOLLOWING:

_____

_____

_____

_____

WHAT WOULD MAKE TODAY GREAT?

_____

_____

AFFIRMATIONS:

_____

_____

_____

HIGHLIGHTS:

_____

_____

_____

LESSONS:

_____

_____

_____

Day 58: ~ Overcoming Fear

"Gratitude shifts your perspective from lack to abundance and allows you to focus on the good in your life, which in turn pulls more goodness into your reality." ~ **Jen Sincero**

Scripture insight:

- **Psalm 28:7 (NIV):** ~ "The Lord is my strength and my shield; my heart trusts in him, and he helps me. My heart leaps for joy, and with my song I praise him."

I AM GRATEFUL FOR THE FOLLOWING:

_____

_____

_____

WHAT WOULD MAKE TODAY GREAT?

_____

_____

_____

AFFIRMATIONS:

_____

_____

_____

HIGHLIGHTS:

_____

_____

_____

LESSONS:

_____

_____

_____

Day 59: ~ Choice Above Circumstances

"Often people ask how I manage to be happy despite having no arms and no legs. The quick answer is that I have a choice. I can be angry about not having limbs, or I can be thankful that I have a purpose. I chose gratitude."
~ **Nick Vujicic.**

Scripture insight:

- **1 Thessalonians 5:16-18 (NIV):** ~ "Rejoice always, pray continually, give thanks in all circumstances; for this is God's will for you in Christ Jesus." -

I AM GRATEFUL FOR THE FOLLOWING:

_____

_____

_____

WHAT WOULD MAKE TODAY GREAT?

_____

_____

_____

AFFIRMATIONS:

_____

_____

_____

HIGHLIGHTS:

_____

_____

_____

LESSONS:

_____

_____

Day 60: ~ Forgiveness and Gratitude

"True forgiveness is when you can say, 'Thank you for that experience.'" ~ **Oprah Winfrey**

Scripture insight:

- **Ephesians 4:32 (NIV):** ~ "Be kind and compassionate to one another, forgiving each other, just as in Christ God forgave you."

I AM GRATEFUL FOR THE FOLLOWING:

_____
_____
_____
_____

WHAT WOULD MAKE TODAY GREAT?

_____
_____
_____
_____

AFFIRMATIONS:

_____
_____
_____

HIGHLIGHTS:

_____
_____
_____

LESSONS:

_____
_____
_____

Day 61: ~ Duty of Thanks

"Gratitude is a duty which ought to be paid, but which none have a right to expect." ~ **Jean-Jacques Rousseau**

Scripture insight:

- **Psalm 95:2 (NIV):** ~ "Let us come before him with thanksgiving and extol him with music and song."

I AM GRATEFUL FOR THE FOLLOWING:

_____

_____

_____

_____

WHAT WOULD MAKE TODAY GREAT?

_____

_____

_____

_____

AFFIRMATIONS:

_____

_____

_____

HIGHLIGHTS:

_____

_____

_____

LESSONS:

_____

_____

_____

Day 62: ~ Commandment of Success

"As with all commandments, gratitude is a description of a successful mode of living. The thankful heart opens our eyes to a multitude of blessings that continually surround us." ~ **James E. Faust**

Scripture insight:

- **Psalm 136:1 (NIV):** ~ "Give thanks to the Lord, for he is good. His love endures forever."

I AM GRATEFUL FOR THE FOLLOWING:

_____
_____
_____

WHAT WOULD MAKE TODAY GREAT?

_____
_____
_____

AFFIRMATIONS:

_____
_____
_____

HIGHLIGHTS:

_____
_____
_____

LESSONS:

_____
_____
_____

Day 63: ~ Infectious Gratefulness

"Gratitude helps you to grow and expand; gratitude brings joy and laughter into your life and into the lives of all those around you." ~ **Eileen Caddy**.

Scripture insight:

- **Proverbs 17:22 (NIV):** ~ "A cheerful heart is good medicine, but a crushed spirit dries up the bones."

I AM GRATEFUL FOR THE FOLLOWING:

_____
_____
_____
_____

WHAT WOULD MAKE TODAY GREAT?

_____
_____
_____

AFFIRMATIONS:

_____
_____
_____

HIGHLIGHTS:

_____
_____
_____

LESSONS:

_____
_____
_____

Day 64: ~ Adversity's Beauty

"Gratitude is an art of painting an adversity into a lovely picture." ~ **Kak Sri**.

Scripture insight:

- **Romans 8:28 (NIV):** ~ "And we know that in all things God works for the good of those who love him, who have been called according to his purpose."

I AM GRATEFUL FOR THE FOLLOWING:

_____
_____
_____
_____

WHAT WOULD MAKE TODAY GREAT?

_____
_____
_____

AFFIRMATIONS:

_____
_____
_____

HIGHLIGHTS:

_____
_____
_____

LESSONS:

_____
_____
_____

Day 65: ~ Sign of Noble Souls

"Gratitude is the sign of noble souls." ~ **Aesop**

Scripture insight:

- **Colossians 3:12 (NIV):** ~ "Therefore, as God's chosen people, holy and dearly loved, clothe yourselves with compassion, kindness, humility, gentleness, and patience."

I AM GRATEFUL FOR THE FOLLOWING:

_____

_____

_____

_____

WHAT WOULD MAKE TODAY GREAT?

_____

_____

_____

_____

AFFIRMATIONS:

_____

_____

_____

HIGHLIGHTS:

_____

_____

_____

LESSONS:

_____

_____

_____

Day 66: ~ Catalyst for Joy

"Gratitude is a powerful catalyst for happiness. It's the spark that lights a fire of joy in your soul." ~ **Amy Collette**

Scripture insight:

- **Proverbs 15:15 (NIV):** ~ "All the days of the oppressed are wretched, but the cheerful heart has a continual feast."

I AM GRATEFUL FOR THE FOLLOWING:

_____
_____
_____
_____

WHAT WOULD MAKE TODAY GREAT?

_____
_____
_____
_____

AFFIRMATIONS:

_____
_____
_____

HIGHLIGHTS:

_____
_____
_____

LESSONS:

_____
_____
_____

Day 67: ~ Life's Splendor

"The more grateful I am, the more beauty I see." ~ **Mary Davis**

Scripture insight:

- **Psalm 34:8 (NIV):** ~ "Oh, taste and see that the Lord is good! Blessed is the man who takes refuge in him!"

I AM GRATEFUL FOR THE FOLLOWING:

_____

_____

_____

_____

WHAT WOULD MAKE TODAY GREAT?

_____

_____

_____

_____

AFFIRMATIONS:

_____

_____

_____

HIGHLIGHTS:

_____

_____

_____

LESSONS:

_____

_____

_____

PART FOUR: ~ FAITH AND TRUST IN DIVINE TIMING

Faith, commitment, and trust are pillars of a spiritual journey, essential in anchoring us during life's highs and lows. Their interplay creates a harmonious path for navigating both spiritual and secular realms. Let's delve deeper.

1. **Faith as the Bedrock**: Faith is an unwavering belief in a power greater than oneself. It's the lens through which we view life's mysteries and the anchor that steadies us in stormy seas.
1. **Commitment: Faith in Action**: Faith isn't passive; it encourages us to live our beliefs. Whether in service, acts of kindness, or the pursuit of justice, our actions become the testament of our faith.
2. **Solace in Trusting God**: When we place our trust in God almighty, we're comforted by the belief that we're not alone. This trust instills strength, especially during turbulent times, reminding us that divine guidance is always at hand.
3. **Embracing Life's Unpredictability**: Challenges are inevitable, but trusting the process means understanding that every event, good or bad, is part of a grander scheme. It's about releasing control and finding peace in the unknown.
4. **Aligning Actions with Values**: To live authentically, our actions should mirror our beliefs. Such alignment fills our journey with purpose and integrity.
5. **Courage & Resilience in Faith**: Faith requires bravery, especially when we face the unknown or adversities. Yet, our trust in God and the process fuels our courage and propels us forward.
6. **Service: The Fruit of Faith & Commitment**: True commitment to faith often manifests as service and compassion. As we touch lives, we enact God's vision for a world filled with kindness.
7. **Striking a Balance**: Life is a dance between effort and surrender. While we do our part, there comes a time to release and trust that God will handle the rest.
8. **The Path to Spiritual Growth**: As we nurture our faith, take committed actions, and place trust in God, we find ourselves evolving spiritually, deepening our connection with God.

9. **Nurturing Hope**: Faith and trust are pillars of hope, assuring us that God's strength is ever-present in our weakness. This hope guides us through challenges, enabling us to emerge gracefully and optimistically.

Essentially, intertwining faith, commitment, and trust enhances a fulfilling life journey. By leaning into these pillars, we find deeper meaning, purpose, and serenity, regardless of life's ebbs and flows.

Day 68: ~ Gratitude for Impact

"We must find time to stop and thank the people who make a difference in our lives." ~ **John F. Kennedy**

Scripture insight:

- **1 Thessalonians 1:2 (NIV):** ~ "We always thank God for all of you and continually mention you in our prayers."

I AM GRATEFUL FOR THE FOLLOWING:

_____
_____
_____
_____

WHAT WOULD MAKE TODAY GREAT?

_____
_____
_____
_____

AFFIRMATIONS:

_____
_____
_____

HIGHLIGHTS:

_____
_____
_____

LESSONS:

_____
_____
_____

Day 69: ~ Eternal Gratitude

"Always have an attitude of gratitude." ~ **Sterling K. Brown**

Scripture insight:

- **Psalm 34:1 (NIV):** ~ "I will extol the Lord at all times; his praise will always be on my lips."

I AM GRATEFUL FOR THE FOLLOWING:

_____
_____
_____
_____

WHAT WOULD MAKE TODAY GREAT?

_____
_____
_____
_____

AFFIRMATIONS:

_____
_____
_____

HIGHLIGHTS:

_____
_____
_____

LESSONS:

_____
_____
_____

Day 70: ~ Seizing Opportunities

"In gratitude, there lies the potential to see opportunities previously unseen." ~ **Urijah Faber**

Scripture insight:

- **Colossians 4:5 (NIV):** ~ "Be wise in the way you act toward outsiders; make the most of every opportunity."

I AM GRATEFUL FOR THE FOLLOWING:

_____
_____
_____
_____

WHAT WOULD MAKE TODAY GREAT?

_____
_____
_____
_____

AFFIRMATIONS:

_____
_____
_____

HIGHLIGHTS:

_____
_____
_____

LESSONS:

_____
_____
_____

Day 71: ~ Path of Reverence

"In moments of gratitude, we find reverence and revelations daily." ~ **John Milton**

Scripture insight:

- **Psalm 19:1 (NIV):** ~ "The heavens declare the glory of God; the skies proclaim the work of his hands."

I AM GRATEFUL FOR THE FOLLOWING:

_____
_____
_____
_____

WHAT WOULD MAKE TODAY GREAT?

_____
_____
_____
_____

AFFIRMATIONS:

_____
_____
_____

HIGHLIGHTS:

_____
_____
_____

LESSONS:

_____
_____
_____

Day 72: ~ Unlimited Thanks

"Gratitude isn't scarce or demanding—it's as plentiful as air. While we effortlessly receive it, we sometimes forget to share it." ~ **Marshall Goldsmith**

Scripture insight:

- **Psalm 100:4 (NIV):** ~ "With gratitude, step into His presence; sing praises to His name."

I AM GRATEFUL FOR THE FOLLOWING:

_____

_____

_____

_____

WHAT WOULD MAKE TODAY GREAT?

_____

_____

_____

AFFIRMATIONS:

_____

_____

_____

HIGHLIGHTS:

_____

_____

_____

LESSONS:

_____

_____

_____

Day 73: ~ Cultivating a Thankful Heart

"Gratitude, like faith, is a muscle. The more you use it, the stronger it grows, and the more power you have to use it on your behalf." ~ **Alan Cohen**

Scripture insight:

- **Psalm 9:1 (NIV):** ~ "I will give thanks to you, Lord, with all my heart; I will tell of all your wonderful deeds."

I AM GRATEFUL FOR THE FOLLOWING:

_____

_____

_____

_____

WHAT WOULD MAKE TODAY GREAT?

_____

_____

_____

AFFIRMATIONS:

_____

_____

_____

HIGHLIGHTS:

_____

_____

_____

LESSONS:

_____

_____

_____

Day 74: ~ Abundance in Thanks

"Gratitude is a currency that we can mint for ourselves and spend without fear of bankruptcy." ~ **Fred De Witt Van Amburgh**

Scripture:

- **2 Corinthians 9:11 (NIV):** ~ "You will be enriched in every way so that you can be generous on every occasion, and through us, your generosity will result in thanksgiving to God."

I AM GRATEFUL FOR THE FOLLOWING:

_____
_____
_____
_____

WHAT WOULD MAKE TODAY GREAT?

_____
_____
_____

AFFIRMATIONS:

_____
_____
_____

HIGHLIGHTS:

_____
_____
_____

LESSONS:

_____
_____
_____

Day 75: ~ Gratitude at Work

"A smart manager will establish a culture of gratitude. Expand the appreciative attitude to suppliers, vendors, delivery people, and of course, customers." — **Harvey Mackay.**

Scripture insight:

- **Philippians 2:3- 4 (NIV):** ~ "Do nothing out of selfish ambition or vain conceit. Rather, **in** humility, value others above yourselves, not looking to your own interests but each of you to the interests of the others."

I AM GRATEFUL FOR THE FOLLOWING:

_____
_____
_____

WHAT WOULD MAKE TODAY GREAT?

_____
_____
_____

AFFIRMATIONS:

_____
_____
_____

HIGHLIGHTS:

_____
_____
_____

LESSONS:

_____
_____

Day 76: ~ Fruits of Thankfulness

"The thankful receiver bears a plentiful harvest." ~ **William Blake.**

Scripture insight:

- **2 Corinthians 9:10 (NIV):** ~ "Now he who supplies seed to the Sower and bread for food will also supply and increase your store of seed and will enlarge the harvest of your righteousness."

I AM GRATEFUL FOR THE FOLLOWING:

_____
_____
_____
_____

WHAT WOULD MAKE TODAY GREAT?

_____
_____
_____
_____

AFFIRMATIONS:

_____
_____
_____

HIGHLIGHTS:

_____
_____
_____

LESSONS:

_____
_____
_____

Day 77: ~ Soulful Nurturing

"Gratitude is the fairest blossom which springs from the soul." ~ **Henry Ward Beecher**

Scripture Insight:

- **Psalm 50:23 (NIV):** ~ "Those who sacrifice thank offerings honor me, and to the blameless I will show my salvation."

I AM GRATEFUL FOR THE FOLLOWING:

_____

_____

_____

_____

WHAT WOULD MAKE TODAY GREAT?

_____

_____

_____

_____

AFFIRMATIONS:

_____

_____

_____

HIGHLIGHTS:

_____

_____

_____

LESSONS:

_____

_____

_____

Day 78: ~ Appreciative Heart

"Gratitude is the sweetest thing in a seeker's life – in all human life. If there is gratitude in your heart, then there will be tremendous sweetness in your eyes." ~ **Sri Chinmoy**

Scriptures:

- **Colossians 3:15 (NIV):** ~ " Let the peace of Christ rule in your hearts, since as members of one body you were called to peace. And be thankful."

I AM GRATEFUL FOR:

_____

_____

_____

WHAT WOULD MAKE TODAY GREAT?

_____

_____

_____

AFFIRMATIONS:

_____

_____

_____

HIGHLIGHTS:

_____

_____

_____

LESSONS:

_____

_____

_____

Day 79: ~ Unlocking Divine Blessings

"When you are grateful - when you can see what you have - you unlock blessings to flow in your life." ~ **Suze Orman**

Scripture insight:

- **Psalm 100:4 (NIV):** ~ "Enter his gates with thanksgiving and his courts with praise; give thanks to him and praise his name."

I AM GRATEFUL FOR:

_____

_____

_____

_____

WHAT WOULD MAKE TODAY GREAT?

_____

_____

_____

_____

AFFIRMATIONS:

_____

_____

_____

HIGHLIGHTS:

_____

_____

_____

LESSONS:

_____

_____

_____

Day 80: ~ A Compass in the Storm

"Gratitude turns negative energy into positive energy. There is no situation or circumstance so small or large that it is not susceptible to gratitude's power. We can start with who we are and what we have today, apply gratitude, then let it work its magic." ~ **Melody Beattie**

Scriptures:

- **Colossians 3:17 (NIV):** ~ "And whatever you do, whether in word or deed, do it all in the name of the Lord Jesus, giving thanks to God the Father through him."

I AM GRATEFUL FOR THE FOLLOWING:

_____
_____
_____

WHAT WOULD MAKE TODAY GREAT?

_____
_____
_____

AFFIRMATIONS:

_____
_____
_____

HIGHLIGHTS:

_____
_____
_____

LESSONS:

_____
_____

Day 81: Consistent Devotion

"Don't pray when it rains if you don't pray when the sun shines." ~ **Leroy Satchel Paige**.

Scripture Insight:

- **1 Thessalonians 5:16- 18 (NIV):** ~ "Rejoice always, pray continually, give thanks in all circumstances; for this is God's will for you in Christ Jesus."

I AM GRATEFUL FOR THE FOLLOWING:

_____

_____

_____

_____

WHAT WOULD MAKE TODAY GREAT?

_____

_____

_____

AFFIRMATIONS:

_____

_____

_____

HIGHLIGHTS:

_____

_____

_____

LESSONS:

_____

_____

_____

Day 82: ~ Balancing Aspiration

"Learn to be thankful for what you already have while you pursue all that you want." ~ **Jim Rohn**

Scripture Insight:

- **Proverbs 16:3 (NIV)** ~ "Commit to the LORD whatever you do, and he will establish your plans."

I AM GRATEFUL FOR THE FOLLOWING:

_____
_____
_____
_____

WHAT WOULD MAKE TODAY GREAT?

_____
_____
_____
_____

AFFIRMATIONS:

_____
_____
_____

HIGHLIGHTS:

_____
_____
_____

LESSONS:

_____
_____
_____

Day 83: ~ New Beginnings

"Don't let negativity from yesterday dull the sparkle of today." ~ **Doreen Virtue**.

Scriptures:

- **Lamentations 3:22-23 (NIV):** ~ "Because of the Lord's great love we are not consumed, for his compassions never fail. They are new every morning; great is your faithfulness."

I AM GRATEFUL FOR THE FOLLOWING:

_____

_____

_____

_____

WHAT WOULD MAKE TODAY GREAT?

_____

_____

_____

AFFIRMATIONS:

_____

_____

_____

HIGHLIGHTS:

_____

_____

_____

LESSONS:

_____

_____

_____

Day 84: ~ Appreciating What You Have

"Now is no time to think of what you do not have. Think of what you can do with what there is." ~ **Ernest Hemingway.**

Scripture insight:

- **Philippians 4:12 (NIV):** ~ "I know what it is to be in need, and I know what it is to have plenty. I have learned the secret of being content in any and every situation, whether well fed or hungry, whether living in plenty or in want."

I AM GRATEFUL FOR THE FOLLOWING:

_____

_____

_____

WHAT WOULD MAKE TODAY GREAT?

_____

_____

_____

AFFIRMATIONS:

_____

_____

_____

HIGHLIGHTS:

_____

_____

_____

LESSONS:

_____

_____

_____

Day 85: ~ Grateful for Life's Simple Blessings

"Got no checkbooks, got no banks. Still, I'd like to express my thanks. I got the sun in the morning and the moon at night." ~ **Irving Berlin**

Scripture insight:

- **Psalm 19:1 (NIV):** ~ "The heavens declare the glory of God; the skies proclaim the work of his hands."

I AM GRATEFUL FOR THE FOLLOWING:

_____
_____
_____
_____

WHAT WOULD MAKE TODAY GREAT?

_____
_____
_____
_____

AFFIRMATIONS:

_____
_____
_____

HIGHLIGHTS:

_____
_____
_____

LESSONS:

_____
_____
_____

Day 86: ~ Belief and Perseverance

"Great things happen to those who don't stop believing, trying, learning, and being grateful." ~ **Alphonse Karr**

Scripture Insight:

- **Psalm 37:4 (NIV):** ~ "Take delight in the Lord, and he will give you the desires of your heart."

I AM GRATEFUL FOR THE FOLLOWING:

_____

_____

_____

_____

WHAT WOULD MAKE TODAY GREAT?

_____

_____

_____

_____

AFFIRMATIONS:

_____

_____

_____

HIGHLIGHTS:

_____

_____

_____

LESSONS:

_____

_____

_____

Day 87: ~ Daily Intentions

"At the end of the day, let there be no excuses, no explanations, no regrets." ~ **Steve Maraboli**

Scripture insight:

- **Psalm 90:12 (NIV)** ~ "Teach us to number our days, that we may gain a heart of wisdom."

I AM GRATEFUL FOR THE FOLLOWING:

_____

_____

_____

_____

WHAT WOULD MAKE TODAY GREAT?

_____

_____

_____

_____

AFFIRMATIONS:

_____

_____

_____

HIGHLIGHTS:

_____

_____

_____

LESSONS:

_____

_____

_____

Day 88: ~ Revealing Potential

"The way to develop the best that is in a person is by appreciation and encouragement." ~ **Charles Schwab**

Scripture insight:

- **1 Thessalonians 5:11 (NIV):** ~ "Therefore encourage one another and build each other up, just as in fact you are doing."

I AM GRATEFUL FOR THE FOLLOWING:

_____
_____
_____
_____

WHAT WOULD MAKE TODAY GREAT?

_____
_____
_____
_____

AFFIRMATIONS:

_____
_____
_____

HIGHLIGHTS:

_____
_____
_____

LESSONS:

_____
_____
_____

Day 89: ~ Mindfulness and Kindness

"Be mindful. Be grateful. Be positive. Be true. Be kind." ~ **Roy T. Bennett**

Scripture insight:

- **Colossians 3:12 (NIV):** ~ "Therefore, as God's chosen people, holy and dearly loved, clothe yourselves with compassion, kindness, humility, gentleness and patience."

I AM GRATEFUL FOR THE FOLLOWING:

_____
_____
_____
_____

WHAT WOULD MAKE TODAY GREAT?

_____
_____
_____
_____

AFFIRMATIONS:

_____
_____
_____

HIGHLIGHTS:

_____
_____
_____

LESSONS:

_____
_____
_____

Day 90: ~ Joy in Divine Timing

"Gratitude for the seemingly insignificant—a seed—this plants the giant miracle." ~ **Ann Voskamp**

Scripture insight:

- **2 Corinthians 9:10 (NIV):** ~ "Now he who supplies seed to the Sower and bread for food will also supply and increase your store of seed and will enlarge the harvest of your righteousness".

I AM GRATEFUL FOR THE FOLLOWING:

_____
_____
_____
_____

WHAT WOULD MAKE TODAY GREAT?

_____
_____
_____

AFFIRMATIONS:

_____
_____
_____

HIGHLIGHTS:

_____
_____
_____

LESSONS:

_____
_____
_____

Conclusion: Embracing Everlasting Gratitude

As we reach the end of our ninety-day journey together, we stand at the threshold of a deep realization. Gratitude, as we've discovered, is far more than a short-lived emotion or a simple 'thank you.' It is a life-changing force that reshapes our perspective, molds our character, and enriches our interactions.

Throughout these pages, we've delved into gratitude's multifaceted essence, uncovering its power to transform both the spiritual and the mundane. We've learned that gratitude doesn't just recognize the good; it amplifies it, turning ordinary moments into extraordinary memories and everyday routines into deeper expressions of joy and contentment.

Remember, each act of thankfulness, whether a quiet prayer or a jubilant celebration, echoes into eternity, affirming our deep connection with God. In gratitude, we find not just practice but a path to a fuller, more connected existence.

As we conclude, I invite you to commit to carrying the lessons of gratitude forward. Let it be a choice, an action, a way of being that continually transforms your life and the lives of those around you.

Epilogue: Charting the Path Forward

As you close this book, I encourage you to pause and reflect on the transformative journey you have embarked upon. Over these ninety days, you've explored the depths of gratitude, faced its challenges, and rejoiced in its joys. This is not just the end of a devotional but the beginning of a lifelong practice.

Reflect on how your understanding of gratitude has evolved:

- Recall the moments or practices that deeply impacted you.
- Consider the positive changes in your attitude, relationships, and outlook.

These reflections are milestones on your path of gratitude. Write them down, cherish them, and revisit them as reminders of your journey.

Now, look ahead. Gratitude is a path that continually unfolds:

- **Integrate Gratitude into Daily Life:** Dedicate daily moments to acknowledge your blessings. Cultivate a habit of thankfulness, whether through morning affirmations or evening reflections.
- **Share the Gift of Gratitude:** Inspire others by sharing your journey. Your story can ignite a spark of gratitude in others, creating a chain of positivity and change.

Gratitude is more than a feeling; it is a choice, a commitment, a way of life. May your heart always resonate with thankfulness, and may your life be a living testament to the boundless power of gratitude.

Appendix: Daily Gratitude Practices:

1. **Gratitude Journaling:** Start or end each day by writing down three things you are grateful for. These could be significant events or small joys.

2. **Gratitude Meditation:** Dedicate a few minutes each day to meditate on what you are thankful for. This can be a quiet reflection or a guided meditation.

3. **Gratitude Walks:** Take a walk, whether in nature or around your neighborhood, and consciously acknowledge the things you see, hear, and feel you are grateful for.

4. **Mealtime Thankfulness:** Before meals, take a moment to express gratitude for the food, the hands that prepared it, and the resources that brought it to your table.

5. **Compliment Diary:** Write down compliments or positive things you said about others and the nice things others said about you. Reflect on these interactions and the feelings they evoke.

6. **Thank You Notes:** Regularly write and send thank-you messages to express appreciation to friends, family, colleagues, or even strangers who made a difference in your day.

7. **Gratitude Jar:** Create a jar where you can drop notes of gratitude each day. Periodically review these notes to remind yourself of the good things in your life.

8. **Acknowledging Others:** Make it a habit to acknowledge verbally and thank people for their help and kindness, however small it may seem.

9. **Daily Gratitude Reminder:** Set a daily reminder on your phone or computer to pause and think of something you're grateful for.

10. **Gratitude Reflection:** End your day by reflecting on a positive experience from the day and why it was meaningful to you.

11. **Grateful Affirmations:** Develop a set of affirmations that reinforce a grateful mindset and repeat them during your morning or evening routine.

12. **Mindful Observation:** Practice mindful observation for a few minutes daily. Focus on a natural or household object and contemplate the aspects of it for which you are grateful.
13. **Volunteering:** Regularly engage in volunteer work or acts of kindness, reflecting on the joy and gratitude these actions bring you and the recipients.
14. **Gratitude Art:** Occasionally, create art, such as a drawing or collage, representing things you are grateful for.
15. **Celebrating Small Wins:** At the end of the day, acknowledge and celebrate your small achievements and the lessons learned from the challenges you faced.

These practices are designed to be flexible and adaptable, allowing individuals to incorporate gratitude into their daily lives in a way that feels natural and beneficial to them.

Made in the USA
Middletown, DE
04 September 2024